LANDSCAPES OF THE CIVIL WAR

THE CHAIR IN WHICH LINCOLN WAS ASSASSINATED. On the night of April 14, 1865, Abraham Lincoln was seated in this upholstered walnut rocking chair watching the comedy *Our American Cousin* from a box overlooking the stage of Ford's Theatre when John Wilkes Booth fired a single, fatal shot into the President's head.

THE STAGE OF FORD'S THEATRE. As a reunited nation confronted the tragic death of its chief executive, scenery for the comedy *Our American Cousin* remained in place on the stage of Ford's Theatre, where Abraham Lincoln was assassinated on Good Friday, 1865.

LANDSCAPES OF THE CIVIL WAR

NEWLY DISCOVERED PHOTOGRAPHS FROM THE

MEDFORD HISTORICAL SOCIETY

EDITED BY CONSTANCE SULLIVAN

PREFACE BY MARK E. NEELY, JR.

INTRODUCTION BY WILLIAM F. STAPP

TEXT BY BRIAN C. POHANKA

A CONSTANCE SULLIVAN BOOK

ALFRED A. KNOPF

NEW YORK 1995

This Is a Borzoi Book
Published by Alfred A. Knopf, Inc.

Published in the United States by Alfred A. Knopf, Inc., New York,
and simultaneously in Canada by Random House Limited, Toronto.
Distributed by Random House, Inc., New York.

Developed, prepared, and produced by Constance Sullivan Editions

ISBN 0-679-44178-6
LC 95-75516

Manufactured in the United States of America

First Edition

PREFACE

MARK E. NEELY, JR.

The military historian John Keegan has observed in his brilliant *History of Warfare* that in 1818 Europe stood peaceful, a "continent disarmed." By 1914, however, nearly every able-bodied European of conscript age owned a military service card with directions to his assigned station for mobilization. Almost every young man, regardless of social class, education, or political persuasion, was ready to march off to the Great War. Paralleling that century of militarization came the development of photography. It seems clear that photography had no deterrent effect on the propensity of civilized nations to go to war.

Yet the earliest interpreters of war photography thought otherwise. Francis Trevelyan Miller, perhaps the first person besides the Civil War cameramen themselves to recognize the lure of the war's photographic record, introduced his landmark ten-volume *Photographic History of the Civil War* in 1911 by pleading that "these photographs are appeals to peace; they are the most convincing evidence of the tragedy of war." The modern reader, enjoying the wisdom of hindsight and knowing that the Marne, the Somme, Verdun, and the other horrors of the Western Front lay only a few years in the future when Mr. Miller wrote, realizes that peace owes little to photographic art.

Put simply, the photographs of dead bodies like those reproduced in these pages *should* have shocked the conscience of nations but apparently did not. That nagging truth makes the job of writing about Civil War photographs awkward. It would ease our conscience to celebrate with a pacific moral veneer the work of Mathew Brady, Alexander Gardner, George Barnard, and the other pioneers of the photojournalism of war. But it doesn't make sense.

In fact, making sense of Civil War photographs in general has not proved easy. Even after more than a century, interpretation remains in its infancy, with but a handful of articles and books on the vast subject and with no work widely recognized as standard or definitive. The task is complicated by the conflicting standards of interpretation. Some regard the photographs as a supplement to the written record of the war, to be interpreted more or less as written records are. Others maintain that the photographs stand on their own as artistic statements. Thus, in addition to the categories of sectionalism, politics, and racism familiarly applied in analyzing written records, for example, the photographs lend themselves to aesthetic interpretation as well. Categories such as landscape, mediation between viewer and objects viewed, and neoclassicism are relevant to understanding them as works of art. Of late, they have been better served by those with an artistic bent, for though they are used as illustrations in many a history book, most of the analysis of photographs has come from the discipline of American studies or from people who work in art galleries. Indeed, the photographs reproduced here were selected on aesthetic grounds rather than to support some narrative of history.

Yet aesthetic and historical standards seem now to be conspiring to bring about an orthodoxy of interpretation that distorts the meaning of the photographs and the history of the war. In these days the term "total war" frequently shows up in learned discussions of Civil War photographs, and increasingly historians assert that the mid-nineteenth-century cameramen documented the advent of "total war." The historical theory of "total war" is familiar to most students of the Civil War, for it is the regnant interpretation of Union victory. This view argues that the North won only when it abandoned the limited war techniques and objectives of the eighteenth century—seizing territory, capturing the enemy's capital, maneuvering to concentrate armies, and respecting civilian lives and property—and instead applied "total war," fighting ceaselessly against the whole of Confederate society, not only its organized armies, but also its economy and its civilians. Typically, the sort of fighting engaged in by William T. Sherman and Ulysses S. Grant provides the focus for this interpretation.

Aesthetic considerations have proved surprisingly easy to reconcile with that historical interpretation. By chance, one of the two great compilations of Civil War photographs put together by photographers immediately after the war focused on scenes from Sherman's campaigns. More important, some writers on Civil War photographs consider the mechanical invention of photography the appropriate medium to portray an industrialized warfare in which the heroic individualism celebrated in traditional battle painting was made irrelevant to victory by increased firepower and range of weaponry and by the calculations of production and supply necessary to keep mass armies in the field. At its simplest, the aesthetic idea embodies the view that an innocent pastoral republic was destroyed, unwittingly, by the cruel industrial methods utilized to bring about Union victory, and that the forward-looking medium of photography ably documented the transformation, while painting, lithography, and engraving languished in the empty heroic categories of the past.

To the degree that such ideas lead us to the pictures and cause us to look at them closely and seek a vocabulary to explain their meaning, they are valuable. And increasingly Civil War photographs *are* interpreted rather than used as mere illustrations. Those interested in them more as historical images, like Alan Trachtenberg, direct our attention, for example, to racial issues. A substantial number of black people appear in Civil War photographs, often to the side of groups and usually in menial roles. These images document not only nineteenth-century racism but also the usually hidden class distinctions in that society. The photographers, after all, took to the field to document war, and yet nineteenth-century American armies had a strangely comfortable view of it, making room for servants for officers. Indeed, Horace Porter, who served on General Grant's staff, in later years boasted that "perhaps no headquarters of a general in supreme command of great armies ever presented so democratic an appearance." But he noted as well that Grant's black servant Bill fetched the general a handful of cigars each morning before he left his tent. Aboard Union ironclad naval vessels of the monitor type—which approached the conditions of submarine service for their crews because so much of the ship remained below water—social class prevailed over fighting efficiency as well; each officer aboard the famous *Monitor*, for example, brought along a personal servant.

As for the aesthetic interpretation, I doubt that any book of Civil War photographs published before very recent times considered "landscapes" as a word appropriate to its title. That is a painterly word, an art criticism word, a word suggestive of beauty and serenity, and less a military term—soldiers call the same physical feature "terrain," and Civil War soldiers treated it with unthinking brutality. To examine the photographs closely in the pages that follow is to see the blasted landscapes of war.

Yet what defiled the Civil War landscapes was only partly industrialized warfare. Nature's real enemy was the ages-old technology of wood and water. Civil War soldiers cooked their food and warmed their chapped hands over wood fires—millions of them. The Union and Confederate armies were customarily idle in winter, when they occupied what were called "winter quarters," usually log huts constructed from what the local forests offered as material—these nineteenth-century soldiers were Daniel Boones more than doughboys.

To be sure, there was more to Civil War-fare than bushwhacking behind trees in the style of the old frontier. Trees fell to the axe to clear fields of fire in ever larger swaths for the more powerful weaponry. And once down, as at Fort Slemmer, the tops of the trees could be laid around the bastion to form a bristling wooden equivalent of barbed wire. Some trees paved the way for industry's intrusions on the landscapes of war. The great wooden trestles kept the railroads running despite enemy destruction of bridges. At any rate, most of the trees felled in these photographs—and there are a great number of them—were probably felled by axe and saw, not by projectiles and explosives.

Though the message of technology and war in the photographs seems mixed, with wood used both for primitive campfires and for railroad trestles, the existing categories of interpretation at least guide us to scan the whole of each photograph carefully, to look at the margins and at what was not necessarily the focus of the photographer. They make us study the images, and think.

But if we think hard, the "total war" interpretation seems hardly satisfactory. Consider the following. Since the photographs in this book were not chosen overtly to convey a narrative of Civil War history, imagine them rearranged, with the portraits of soldiers and the wide views of drill placed at the end of the book and the skeletal walls of burned-out Richmond, the ruined classicism of Charleston, and the brick chimney of Falmouth, Virginia, placed at the beginning of the book. The actual dates of these famous photographs of architectural destruction do range from 1863 to 1865, even though they appear as a category of ruins all in one place, at the end of the volume. What idea would the reader come away with if the photographs were thus arranged? Surely the photographs would not seem necessarily to prove that the war became more indiscriminately destructive.

It is not my role to answer such questions in a merely suggestive preface but rather to pose them, and in so doing to call into question easy answers to the meaning of Civil War photographs. Any survey of the available archives of photography will reveal that the individual officer or soldier, armed with a musket and bayonet or saber, holds the premier position as subject, because of the decentralized nature of the enterprise. For Civil War photography was primarily that—free enterprise—and to make their living, most photographers camped out near the armies and made portraits for the soldiers to send home to their families and friends. These mostly indoor, studio-bound formal poses greatly outnumber the outdoor panoramas and landscapes.

Among the relatively scarcer outdoor images, technology figured rather prominently for several reasons peculiar to photography rather than to warfare in the middle of the nineteenth century. The photographers could not get near combat and did not need to, because their cameras could not capture moving subjects. Besides soldiers in uniform alone or in small groups, the military subjects available far to the rear, where Civil War photographers of necessity congregated, tended to favor transportation and supply. Even artillery, with its superior range and more fixed position, garnered disproportionate attention. Much of the real war was conducted at musket range—the length of a football field—by individuals on foot firing hand-held weapons, and these do not figure as prominently in outdoor photographs. Moreover, technological subjects were favored because the government—or rather the army—was slow to recognize the uses of photography, leaving the technologically minded engineers to capitalize on the medium most fully. Thus the photographs taken with a professional purpose of illustrating military technology gained government funding and scrupulous official care in preservation. They hold greater sway among the surviving outdoor views than they deserve as representations of the nature of warfare in the 1860s.

In addition to abandoning the "total war," industrialized viewpoint in examining the Medford archive of Civil War photographs, I would recommend keeping in mind five considerations. First, there was no official government photography except for technical purposes connected to engineering, topographical production, and supply: propaganda was essentially unknown to Civil War governments (apart from the ordinary occasions of politics and elections). In fact, one of the photographs' most important, though often unstated, appeals lies in their innocence. Nevertheless, their exemption from the loathsome corruption of government attempts to manipulate public opinion does not make them somehow candid, truthful, and random. A second point, then, made best by photographic historian William Frassanito, is that scenes are sometimes artfully posed and often carefully selected. The photographers' secrets of composition have not been readily and openly revealed to us because—and this is the third point to remember in interpreting Civil War photographs—they constituted commerce rather than journalism. Photography was more a business than an art. Recordkeeping was poor; these men were primarily making money, not history. Few photographers, if any, were directly tied to news organizations. Most were what we might call freelancers, trying to capture images to sell to ordinary citizens or to the soldiers themselves for money to put food on the table. Innocent, but posed and commercial, these images hardly sound as though they would embody the quality to make them endlessly fascinating—indeed, more fascinating the farther they recede in time. One often-overlooked explanation of their enduring value and extremely high quality is that they were, nearly every one, taken by professionals; that is the fourth point. Amateur photography was rare enough in the age before flexible film, and, near the battlefields, nonexistent.

The fifth point has received perhaps the least emphasis in the existing literature on Civil War photography. All of the considerations mentioned thus far concern the origin, creation, composition, and purpose of photography. One should think as well of the uses to which Civil War photographs were put at the time. Here the knowledge of collectors is as important as that of scholars. Those who frequent trade shows and patronize dealers in Americana recognize immediately the characteristic repository of antique Civil War photographs: a leather-covered album, often ornately decorated with embossing, metal studs, and gilt tooling, containing thick cardboard pages with open windows on each page into which photographs could be slotted. The standard photograph to fit these parlor albums was the roughly two-by-four-inch *carte de visite* (usually called "c.d.v."), a paper image mounted on a stiff card about the size of a nineteenth-century calling card. If wars tend to have their characteristic medium of visual representation—the newsreel for World War II, for example—the characteristic medium for the American Civil War was the *carte de visite* photograph.

Surviving albums in which the order of arrangement has not been altered since the Civil War era often begin with a photograph of the

President, Abraham Lincoln, followed by portraits of other notable politicians, followed in turn by those of famous generals and heroes of the war. Some contain landscapes of war reproduced in these pages. At the back of the album one finds various unrecognizable people—men in captains' uniforms, women, boys, and girls. The family was relegated in these parlor albums to the back of the pantheon of celebrity, which is perhaps indicative of the true priorities of that era. Public causes came first, as can be proved by the unparalleled voter turnout of the era (in the 1860 election, which precipitated the war, an estimated 82 percent of eligible voters actually voted in Northern states, and the figure was almost as high in the disaffected South). The vast Civil War armies of men, almost all of them volunteers, rushed to the colors and then died in numbers that today would be considered unconscionable: more than 25 percent of those who served in the Confederate army died in the war. Americans have never fought harder, and by and large they volunteered to do it. They were never more dedicated to public causes and less preoccupied by private concerns.

It seems little wonder, then, that Civil War photographs were so plentiful. They satisfied curiosity and testified to patriotism. The latter should not be underestimated. Even in 1866, when Alexander Gardner and George Barnard produced their deluxe collector's editions of large-format photographs mounted, captioned, and bound in albums, they did not reach beyond the narrowest bounds of patriotism. Barnard's *Photographic Views of Sherman's Campaign*, for example, begins with a studio group portrait of Sherman and his most important subordinates, taken after the war, apparently, in Washington, D.C., and follows with images of various sites of the military campaign, with views of Charleston, South Carolina, thrown in for narrative and vindictive completeness. (As Keith F. Davis, the most knowledgeable modern student of Barnard, has noted, Sherman actually bypassed the city, but Yankees hated the city and the state for starting the war and wanted to see them destroyed.)

Barnard did not include in his album a photograph of either of Sherman's famous opponents, Confederate generals Joseph E. Johnston and John Bell Hood. Even if authorial purity dictated that he exclude photographs taken by others—as presumably the wartime portraits of the enemy's generals would have been—Barnard might have sought out Hood or Johnston on his tour of the South after the war, when he revisited the fields to round out his compilation of important sites for his album. He did not. Almost nobody in the North was ready yet to have Hood's or Johnston's likeness sitting on the parlor table, as though they were among the honored household saints.

Likewise, *Gardner's Photographic Sketch Book of the War*, published in two volumes and costing a whopping $150, included a photograph of President Lincoln, taken while he visited General George B. McClellan after the battle of Antietam, but had no other hero to celebrate. Gardner patriotically excluded Confederate heroes, and when he spoke of "willing sacrifice to the cause" in the beginning of his book, he meant the Union cause specifically, not the abstract idea of sacrifice to any ideal. His captions offered a curious mixture of the high-minded Victorian language of sacrifice (the sort of language that World War I and Ernest Hemingway made forever ridiculous) and vulgar anecdotalism. In identifying what might be taken as a shocking meditation on death, a photograph of a burial detail on the old Bull Run battlefield, Gardner's book mentioned the discovery of a glass eye rattling around in one of the unburied skulls!

From curious detail to sublime aesthetic, photographs of the Civil War have always offered viewers a wealth of material for interpretation, but they have not always been popular. Apparently no one attempted to put together professional albums for sale after Gardner's and Barnard's now-famous efforts, both produced in 1866. Gradually, the purchase and mounting in albums of war heroes' images must have slackened in pace. Contemporary writing about the war photographs is extremely sparse: a famous article by New England intellectual Oliver Wendell Holmes, published in *The Atlantic Monthly* in July 1863, is quoted again and again in articles on Civil War photographs because it offers about the only major consideration of the subject by anyone before the twentieth century. Use and study of the photographs was impeded by the lack of technology to reproduce them in printing, until the late 1880s. Even then there seems to have been no major reconsideration of the photographic record, although the war itself had been undergoing extensive interpretation and reminiscence in books and magazines from 1880 on. Not until the fiftieth anniversary of the war's outbreak, in 1911, did Francis Trevelyan Miller recognize the value of the nation's historic trove of Civil War photographs.

Historic photographs are undervalued no longer, as anyone knows who has attended an auction of them in recent years. But Civil War photographs remain underinterpreted and dimly understood. Perhaps the Medford collection, properly preserved and presented for public scrutiny, as it must be, will inspire the carefully exhaustive study these remarkable relics deserve.

NOTE

DR. JOSEPH VALERIANI

PRESIDENT, MEDFORD HISTORICAL SOCIETY

The city of Medford, Massachusetts, six miles north of Boston, was settled in the 1630s and has a long, rich history. In 1896, the Medford Historical Society was organized as a repository for objects and images reflecting life in Medford through the years, and in 1916 the society moved into its present headquarters and museum on Governor's Avenue. Groups of schoolchildren frequently visit the museum, and in 1990 one of those students went home and told his father, Noah Dennen, about the interesting collection of Civil War artifacts he had seen there. Mr. Dennen, a Civil War buff, soon visited the museum himself, and Michael Bradford, the society's librarian and curator, showed him a collection of Civil War photographs that had been stored for years in a wooden chest on the top floor of the building. Astonished by the number and quality of the photographs and the fact that he had never seen many of them before, Mr. Dennen quickly suspected that the collection might be of interest to Civil War historians. He invited Brian Pohanka, an expert on the Civil War, to view the photographs, and six hours later, black to the elbow with dust and dirt, Mr. Pohanka confirmed Mr. Dennen's suspicion: the chest contained one of the largest and finest collections of Civil War photographs in existence—fifty-four hundred prints in all.

The collection, it turned out, had been amassed by General Samuel Crocker Lawrence, commander of the Lawrence Light Guard during the war and later mayor of Medford. Upon General Lawrence's death, in 1911, the collection passed into the custody of the Light Guard, and in 1948 Colonel John J. Carew of the guard and Mrs. U. Haskell Crocker, General Lawrence's granddaughter, donated the chestful of photographs to the Medford Historical Society.

When *The Boston Globe* and *Civil War Times Illustrated* announced the discovery of the Medford collection, the society was besieged with requests to examine or purchase the photographs. A handful of historians and curators of photography were allowed to see the collection, and they agreed unanimously on its importance. Gordon Baldwin, of the Getty Museum, wrote that "the Medford hoard of photographs is without doubt one of the most important collections in this country of prints made from the original negatives of some of the most important photographers of the Civil War."

The Medford Historical Society, now aware that it possessed a priceless collection, moved the photographs to a vault at the Medford Cooperative Bank and formed a committee to decide what to do with them. The committee, composed of Dr. Carl Seaburg, Stephen Johnson, Carol Sbuttoni, Jay Griffin, Michael Bradford, Noah Dennen, and myself, agreed that the collection would not be sold, would remain in Medford, and would be made available to Civil War scholars after the photographs had been properly conserved. Although the photographs were visually in superb condition, most of the albumen prints had never been mounted on cardboard, and many of them had curled and needed careful physical conservation. For two years, the society raised funds to begin this effort. About nine hundred of the photographs have now been conserved at the Northeast Document Conservation Center in Andover, Massachusetts, and income from this book will be used to continue the conservation effort.

Until the collection is conserved, we have, regrettably, had to turn down the many, many requests we have received to view the photographs. A few photographs were exhibited at Tufts University during the inauguration of President John DiBiaggio, but except for that exhibit, *Landscapes of the Civil War* represents the first public opportunity to see a selection of the remarkable photographs General Lawrence assembled in the years after the Civil War. It is also a first step toward making the entire collection accessible to anyone with an interest in this momentous period in our nation's history.

INTRODUCTION

WILLIAM F. STAPP

The photographs in this book were selected from an extraordinary collection of approximately five thousand original albumen prints recently discovered by the Medford, Massachusetts, Historical Society. The collection was assembled after the Civil War by Samuel Crocker Lawrence, a wealthy Medford businessman who commanded the Lawrence Light Guard, the town's militia unit. At the first battle of Bull Run, he was wounded while leading Company E of the Fifth Massachusetts Infantry. He became a general in the Massachusetts Militia in 1862, and played a prominent role in state military affairs for the rest of his life. When Lawrence died in 1911, his Civil War photographs were turned over to the Lawrence Light Guard, who, in 1948, bequeathed them to the Medford Historical Society, which stored the prints in a chest in the attic, where they were discovered in 1990. One of the most extensive collections of original Civil War photographs to survive, this is also one of the most distinguished, owing to the exceptionally fine condition of the prints.

These photographs were selected because of the visual impact of their images as well as their superb print quality. They are arranged according to aesthetic considerations rather than chronology; there is no implied narrative content. Though the selection suggests the range, variety, and affective power of Civil War photography, it was neither conceived nor organized as a record of the conflict. To those who know the photographs of the war primarily through black-and-white reproductions in books and magazines, or even through typical vintage prints, which are usually yellowed and faded, the deep color and rich tones of these reproductions, which are close to those of the original photographs, should be a revelation. No matter how horrific their subject matter, the beauty of these prints is overwhelming.

Although the Civil War was not the first military conflict to be photographed, it was the first significant historical event to be witnessed to a substantial degree by the camera. In 1861, the profession of photography was little more than twenty years old, and photographic technology had barely evolved to the point where documenting events was a realistic possibility. Americans had eagerly embraced photography when it was introduced from Europe in 1839, but enthusiasts adopted the daguerreotype process rather than any of the other early photographic technologies and established a successful studio industry that depended on it. Consequently, American photographers were reluctant to use the more flexible forms of photography that were introduced from the mid-1840s on. By 1851, the daguerreotype had become obsolete in Europe, but it continued to dominate American photography for a few more years, until the major studios finally began to make the transition to the wet-collodion process. Even then, the conventions and practices of the earlier period continued to prevail. Until 1861, American photography was primarily formal portrait photography executed in a studio; outdoor photographs of any sort were very rarely made east of the Mississippi River. When the Civil War began, the technology and the special skills to document it photographically had only recently become familiar to American photographers, and very few of them had any practical experience with the real difficulties of making photographs in the field.

One of the few who did possess both technical expertise and practical experience was Alexander Gardner, a Scotsman who had immigrated to the United States in 1856. Gardner, who had learned photography in Glasgow, found immediate employment with the photographic entrepreneur Mathew Brady in New York, undoubtedly because he was expert at the wet-collodion process. Also an accomplished businessman, Gardner took over the management of Brady's books and stabilized his finances, which had been in a precarious condition for some years, in spite of Brady's eminence. In 1858, when Brady decided to establish a studio in Washington, D.C., he sent Gardner to run it.

Although Brady later claimed (and is still popularly given) credit for both conceiving and implementing the idea of photographically documenting the Civil War, Alexander Gardner was more likely to have had this inspiration. Brady and other American photographers were well aware that the Britons Roger Fenton and James Robertson had made photographs during the Crimean War (1853–1856), under extremely difficult conditions, but Gardner was perhaps the only photographer in the United States who had actually had an opportunity to see Fenton's Crimean War photographs, since the work had been widely exhibited in Great Britain in 1855. Gardner was, therefore, probably the only photographer in the United States who truly understood the potential of the camera to document warfare. Whether or not he actually thought of creating a photographic record of the Civil War, he undoubtedly encouraged Brady to undertake the project as a commercial venture. In the end, Gardner emerged as one of the most significant photographers of the conflict.

The outbreak of war proved an immediate boon to the American photographic industry, which had suffered from a decreased demand for its products since the worldwide depression of 1857. As one British reporter noted in 1862, "America swarms with the members of the mighty tribe of cameristas, and the civil war has developed their business in the same way that it has given an impetus to the manufacturers of metallic air-tight coffins and embalmers of the dead. The Young Volunteer rushes off at once to the studio when he puts on his uniform, and the soldier of a year's campaign sends home his likeness that the absent ones may see what changes have been produced in him by war's alarms." The overwhelming majority of Civil War images were portraits of soldiers, taken by hundreds of photographers in local towns or in temporary studios near the troops' encampments. So many soldiers' portraits were taken that early in the war the postal system ground to a halt because of the number and weight of photographic likenesses being sent through the mails. Toward the end of the war, the federal government belatedly acknowledged the enormous scale of this photographic commerce by imposing a temporary sales tax on photographic prints.

While the portrait record of the Civil War provided comprehensive documentation of the enlisted men and officers, at least for the Union armies, documentation of the war itself was necessarily more sporadic. For one thing, only a few photographers were actively engaged in photographing the scenes and events of the conflict. Just four men—Alexander Gardner, Timothy O'Sullivan, George N. Barnard, and Andrew J. Russell, the only Civil War photographer who actually held military rank—were responsible for most of the photographs. James Gardner (Alexander's brother), James F. Gibson, Thomas C. Roche, David Knox, David Woodbury, John Reekie, and several others also took war views, and their work is also represented in these pages, but with the exception of Russell, all of these men were either employed by Mathew Brady or associated with Alexander Gardner after he left Brady's service in 1862. Barnard's most important contribution, his documentation of Sherman's 1864 campaign across Tennessee, Georgia, and South Carolina, was begun after he separated from Gardner.

A number of war views were produced under Brady's aegis and credited to him between 1861 and 1865, but his personal contribution to the photography of the war was actually minimal. He himself did not work the camera; in a brief biography written in 1851, Charles Lester commented that Brady suffered from a severe, chronic visual impairment resulting from a childhood illness and could not see well enough to focus an image on the ground glass. His attempt to photograph the first battle of Bull Run, in July 1861, was so disastrous that he did not return to a major battlefield until July 1863, when he supervised a series of photographs at Gettysburg a week after the fighting there. Brady's only other significant appearance in the war zone before Lee's surrender was in the summer of 1864, when he spent parts of June and July photographing the Union troops besieging Petersburg, Virginia.

In four years of fighting, this small group of photographers produced a total of between six and ten thousand negatives of war views. Almost all of these record military life and activity behind the Union lines; a minority —several hundred plates, at most—relate to battles and combat. None documents an actual engagement. Comprehensive photographic coverage of the war was restricted by the practical limitations of the technology and by the problems of transporting the photographers' bulky, fragile equipment and supplies.

One difficulty was that the wet-collodion process required the photog-rapher to coat and sensitize his glass plates on the spot, just before making his exposure, and to process them immediately before the tacky emulsion —the wet collodion—dried out. This meant he needed instant access to a darkroom, a problem which most Civil War photographers resolved by outfitting a special wagon as a portable darkroom, the famous "whatizzit" wagon. It also prevented virtually any spontaneous response to an event. A second problem was the plates' relative insensitivity to light; they had to be exposed for so long that motion was blurred, and a figure that moved too quickly into or out of range was recorded as a faint, ghostly image. Not only was it useless to attempt to photograph action, but photographers working their cameras in an exposed position made themselves targets for enemy shellfire. Another obstacle was the thick haze of gun smoke that quickly obscured the battlefield during an engagement. Since both artillery pieces and small arms were charged with black powder, which creates a cloud of dense white smoke when it detonates, visibility was often limited to a few yards during heavy action.

As a consequence of all these factors, photographers were effectively restricted to photographing the aftermaths of battles rather than the battles themselves. These photographs, however, are among the most potent visual documents of war ever made. Alexander Gardner's images of Confederate corpses at Antietam, his and Timothy O'Sullivan's views of Union and Confederate casualties at Gettysburg, and Thomas C. Roche's studies of Confederate bodies in the trenches before Petersburg remain, in Oliver Wendell Holmes's words, "a commentary on civilization such as a savage might well triumph to show its missionaries." Gardner's photographs from Antietam, first displayed at Brady's New York gallery in 1862, were the first photographs of war dead that most Americans had ever seen, and the brutal, unsentimental images stunned a public whose concepts of warfare derived from highly romanticized paintings and prints.

Photography of the war was also influenced by logistics and geography. Most of the photographers worked in the East, primarily in Virginia east of the Shenandoah Valley, but also in Maryland and Pennsylvania. These areas were easily accessible from Washington (where both Brady and Gardner maintained their studios) by rail, waterways, and a network of relatively good roads, and the distances were not vast; Richmond, the Confederate capital, is about 110 miles south of Washington, and Gettysburg is just 70 miles to the north. This meant that studio headquarters and the photographers in the field could communicate fairly easily, speedily exchanging supplies, negatives, and news of the latest developments. Moreover, since the war in the East was being fought in the North's backyard, there was naturally a greater interest in the campaigns there.

Political connections, luck, perseverance, and access to transportation also played a role in determining who photographed what. Captain Andrew J. Russell was assigned to document the accomplishments of the U.S. Military Railroad and consequently took pictures along the rail lines in Virginia, which took him to the second battle of Fredericksburg, in April 1863, and to the final attack on Petersburg and Richmond in April 1865. George N. Barnard, who began the war in Brady's employ and later associated himself with Alexander Gardner, was appointed official photographer of the chief engineer's office of the Division of Mississippi, which gave him access to the military trains that supplied General Sherman's army. In 1864 and 1865, he was able to produce numerous carefully composed, large-format views of significant points along the route of General Sherman's March to the Sea, returning in 1866 to complete the series. That same year he published sixty-one of these photographs as *Photographic Views of Sherman's Campaign*, a work that ranks in historical significance with Gardner's *Sketch Book of the War,* also published in 1866.

Gardner's war photography was intermittent, but because he was attached to General George McClellan's staff as a civilian employee, he was probably with the Army of the Potomac during the battle of Antietam, in September 1862, and was able to photograph after the Confederate forces had retreated. He and O'Sullivan apparently followed General George Meade's army into Pennsylvania in anticipation of a major clash, and they arrived in time to take their unforgettable views of Gettysburg; Brady, who must have decided to go to Gettysburg after news of the victory reached Washington, did not arrive until a week later.

Both O'Sullivan and Roche spent most of the war in the field, which gave them access to scenes of army camp life as well as practical experience with combat. O'Sullivan took pains to make a number of images of Union soldiers at drill during the Fredericksburg and Chancellorsville campaigns. By the time Roche was shelled by Rebel cannon at the Dutch Gap canal, he had witnessed enough fighting to know that no two shots would hit the same spot, so he simply moved his camera into the shell hole from the first shot fired at him and continued to take photographs.

In contrast to the relatively extensive coverage of the war in the East, very few photographs document the war waged in the Gulf, along the Mississippi, or in the West. Even Grant's capture of Vicksburg, which established final Union control over the South's most vital supply route, the Mississippi River, and simultaneously split the Confederacy, was not photographed. With the exception of Barnard's work in the South, the major photographic activity of the conflict occurred within a relatively narrow corridor running from Gettysburg in the north to Richmond in the south and from the Atlantic seaboard on the east to the Shenandoah Mountains in the west.

The photographs in this book reflect all the limitations imposed by geography, technology, politics, and the like, yet they remain a powerfully evocative tribute to the skill and determination of the Civil War photographers. The fact that these extraordinary images were essentially forgotten in an obscure attic for nearly eighty years, so that they were not handled or exposed to light, provides us with the opportunity to see them much as the American public first did.

PLATES

FORT JOHNSON, JAMES ISLAND, SOUTH CAROLINA. Fort Johnson, a Confederate bastion on James Island, South Carolina, was one of numerous earthworks constructed for the defense of Charleston Harbor. Armed with nearly thirty massive cannon, Fort Johnson defied capture until its evacuation in February 1865. The battered rampart of Fort Sumter, where the first shots of the war were fired, is visible in the distance.

CAMP McDOWELL, ARLINGTON HEIGHTS, VIRGINIA. In the summer of 1861, military engineers of Company K, Eighth New York State Militia, gathered in front of their captain's tent at Camp McDowell, Virginia. Like many other Federal militia units, the Eighth New York marched to war clad in uniforms of gray.

CONFEDERATE DEAD, MARYE'S HEIGHTS, FREDERICKSBURG. MAY 3, 1863. On May 4, 1863, Captain Andrew J. Russell recorded the grim aftermath of a successful Union assault at Fredericksburg, Virginia. Mississippians slain on the preceding day are sprawled amid the debris of battle at the foot of Marye's Heights.

PAGES 30–31. SOLDIERS OF THE FOURTH MICHIGAN INFANTRY. The volunteers of the Fourth Michigan Infantry had yet to "see the elephant" (soldier slang for the baptism of fire) when they posed for a cameraman in their encampment on the outskirts of Washington, D.C., in the summer of 1861. By the end of their three-year term of enlistment, nearly half of the thirteen hundred men who served with the Fourth Michigan had been killed or wounded.

Capt. Russell Phot

CHECKING ORDERS AT FORT RICHARDSON, VIRGINIA. With his field officers and orderlies looking on, Colonel Robert O. Tyler, First Connecticut Heavy Artillery, examines a dispatch delivered to the garrison of Fort Richardson, one of the earthen fortifications guarding the approaches to Washington, D.C.

OFFICERS OF THE FIFTY-FIFTH NEW YORK INFANTRY AT FORT GAINES. Officers of the Fifty-fifth New York, a colorfully garbed regiment recruited among Manhattan's French immigrants, stand beside a mammoth 32-pounder cannon on the ramparts of Fort Gaines, on the Washington–Maryland border. Colonel Philippe Régis de Trobriand, pointing from his perch on the big gun, had been the editor of New York's French newspaper, *Courier des Etats-Unis.*

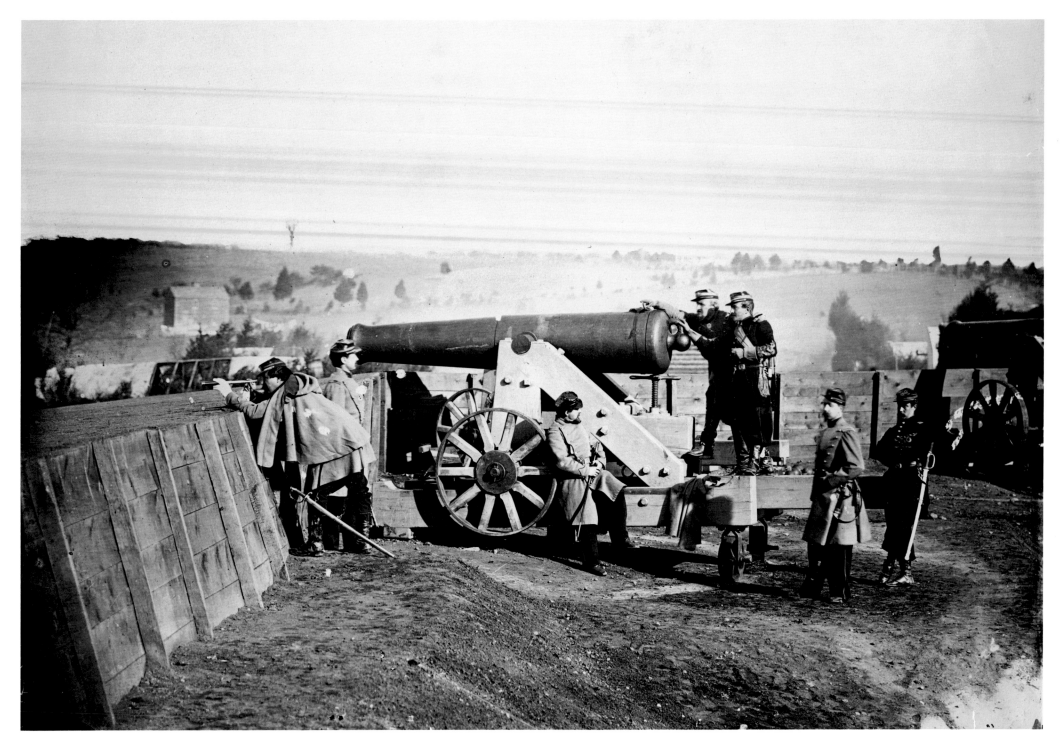

SOLDIERS OF THE SECOND PENNSYLVANIA HEAVY ARTILLERY AT FORT SLEMMER. Troops of the Second Pennsylvania Heavy Artillery march through the sally port of Fort Slemmer. With four cannon and a perimeter of only ninety-three yards, Fort Slemmer was one of the smaller earthworks in the Washington defenses.

OFFICERS AND TROOPERS OF THE SEVENTH NEW YORK CAVALRY NEAR WASHINGTON, WINTER 1861–62. Brigadier General Innis N. Palmer (third from left) visits the camp of the Seventh New York Cavalry during the daily ritual of dress parade. Military ceremonies, conducted in strict accordance with army regulations, were intended to foster discipline, deportment, and unit pride.

THE SEVENTH PENNSYLVANIA RESERVES AT DRILL NEAR LANGLEY, VIRGINIA. Marching in a column of companies led by their regimental band, troops of the Seventh Pennsylvania Reserves begin the daily battalion drill near their camp at Langley, Virginia. The complex choreography of Civil War tactics required almost superhuman precision from the individual soldiers. In the winter of 1861–62, the Union Army of the Potomac trained relentlessly for the inevitable bloodletting that would come with the spring.

UNION WINTER CAMP NEAR CULPEPER, VIRGINIA. The white canvas tents and log huts of a Union encampment stand in a desolate landscape near Culpeper, Virginia, where the Army of the Potomac passed the winter of 1863–64.

PASS IN THE RACCOON RANGE, WHITESIDE, TENNESSEE. A detachment of Federal troops guard a strategic bridge on the Nashville and Chattanooga Railroad at Whiteside, Tennessee. The nearby city of Chattanooga was a Union supply base and a staging point for General Sherman's campaign against Atlanta.

OFFICERS OF THE 164TH AND 170TH NEW YORK NEAR FAIR-
FAX, VIRGINIA. Officers of the 164th and 170th New York, part of an Irish-
American brigade known as the Corcoran Legion, gather at a woodcutters'
camp near Fairfax, Virginia. The following summer, Colonel James P.
McMahon (arms folded, second from left) was killed carrying his regi-
ment's flag onto the Confederate earthworks at the battle of Cold Harbor.

UNION OFFICER IN WALL TENT. A black attendant holds the horse of a Union officer, who lounges in his shirtsleeves in front of a wall tent. The sides of the tent have been raised to alleviate the summer heat.

WINTER QUARTERS OF REGIMENTAL BUTCHER. Salted sides of beef are hung up to dry in a regimental commissary tent at a Federal winter camp. Beef proved a welcome relief from the standard ration of salt pork, dubbed "sowbelly" by the men in the ranks.

UNION QUARTERMASTER EMPLOYEES ABOARD A SUPPLY BOAT. Civilian quartermaster employees relax aboard a Union supply boat. In both the eastern and western theaters of the war, rivers were crucial arteries of transport for feeding and equipping the armies.

WARD IN ARMORY SQUARE HOSPITAL, WASHINGTON, D.C. Nurses and medical orderlies attend wounded soldiers in one of the large wards of a Washington, D.C., military hospital. Patients found the clean linen and patriotic decor cheering, in contrast to the filthy front-line field hospitals.

51

FREEDMEN'S VILLAGE. As Federal armies battled their way through the Confederacy, tens of thousands of slaves found deliverance from bondage. Awaiting an uncertain future, many former slaves lived in ramshackle shantytowns called freedmen's villages.

CAMP ON U.S. MILITARY RAILROAD, CITY POINT, VIRGINIA. In June 1864, City Point, at the confluence of the Appomattox and James rivers, became the principal supply base for General Grant's drive against Petersburg and Richmond. The U.S. Military Railroad bore food and ammunition from the docks to the front lines.

CHATTANOOGA, TENNESSEE. Union encampments sprawl across the denuded slopes of Cameron Hill above the strategic city of Chattanooga, Tennessee. Of vital importance as both a river and a rail center, Chattanooga was the scene in November 1863 of U. S. Grant's crushing victory over the Confederate forces of General Braxton Bragg.

CONSTRUCTING A STOCKADE AT ALEXANDRIA, VIRGINIA. Black laborers erect a palisaded stockade to protect the Union railroad depot at Alexandria, Virginia. Though Alexandria's roundhouse and rail yards were well inside the circle of forts guarding Washington and its environs, fear of Confederate raiding parties prompted Federal authorities to limit access to them.

LABORERS AT THE ALEXANDRIA WHARF. The contribution of African-Americans to the Union war effort was substantial. While nearly two hundred thousand black soldiers and sailors served in uniform, many others worked on the wharves and at the railroad depots that supplied Northern forces in the field.

UPPER WHARF AT BELLE PLAIN, VIRGINIA. CONFLUENCE OF POTOMAC CREEK AND POTOMAC RIVER. In the spring of 1864, Belle Plain Landing, nine miles northwest of Fredericksburg, Virginia, became the principal base for Grant's ambitious offensive against General Robert E. Lee's Army of Northern Virginia. Wounded Federals, captured Confederates, and thousands of tons of supplies were processed there.

Bry Plain
Pontoon Bridge erected by
15 Corps
Gen Benham Chief
May 15. 1864

59

WHITE HOUSE LANDING, PAMUNKEY RIVER. During the initial stages of General George McClellan's ultimately unsuccessful attempt to take Richmond in the spring of 1862, White House Landing, on the Pamunkey River, served as a Yankee supply depot. Two years later, it filled this role again, when Grant's army battled its way southward.

MONITOR *SAUGUS*, JAMES RIVER. Equipped with a torpedo net, the Civil War version of a minesweeper, the monitor *Saugus* was one of a fleet of Federal ironclad warships that operated on Virginia's James River. The *Saugus* later served as a temporary prison for suspected conspirators in the plot to assassinate President Lincoln.

EARTHWORKS AT PETERSBURG, VIRGINIA. More than nine months of siege and battle left the environs of Petersburg, Virginia, a shell-torn wasteland. Some ninety thousand men were killed, wounded, or missing in action before the Confederate stronghold fell to General Grant's Federal forces.

WINTER VIEW OF CAVALRY STABLES, GIESBORO POINT, D.C. (PANORAMA). A recent snowfall lends an air of enchantment to army stables near Fort Carroll, at Giesboro Point, Washington, D.C. Much of the Federal cavalry drew horses from the Giesboro remount depot.

PAGE 67. U.S. MILITARY RAILROAD ENGINE AT APPROACH TO UNION MILLS, VIRGINIA. U.S. Military Railroad locomotives approach a water tank and storage area at Union Mills, Virginia, where the Orange and Alexandria Railroad crossed Bull Run. The line was a vital north-south link between Washington, D.C., and the troops in the field.

PAGE 68. TRANSPORT *MISSIONARY* ON THE TENNESSEE RIVER, CHATTANOOGA. During the tenacious Confederate siege of Chattanooga in the autumn of 1863, Tennessee River transports like the *Missionary* were able to maintain a precarious supply line to the Union garrison.

PAGE 69. CITY POINT AFTER EXPLOSION OF ORDNANCE BARGES. Splintered timbers and other debris litter the docks at City Point, Virginia, following the explosion of an ordnance barge on August 9, 1864. Ignited by Confederate saboteurs, the blast claimed the lives of forty-three laborers, and General Grant himself narrowly escaped injury.

U.S. LOCOMOTIVE ON BRIDGE OVER BULL RUN AT UNION MILLS. The Orange and Alexandria Railroad bridge over Bull Run at Union Mills was destroyed by Confederate forces and rebuilt by the Union several times in the course of the war.

TRESTLE BRIDGE AT WHITESIDE, TENNESSEE. In 1864, Union engineers spanned the valley of Running Water Creek near Whiteside, Tennessee, with a 780-foot-long railroad trestle. Photographer George N. Barnard, who was employed by General Sherman's chief engineer, made this view of the delicate-looking structure.

RUINS OF CONFEDERATE TRAIN IN ATLANTA, GEORGIA. When General John Bell Hood's Confederate forces evacuated Atlanta on September 1, 1864, an ammunition-laden freight train was put to the torch so that it would not fall into Yankee hands. The resulting explosion obliterated the boxcars and a nearby mill.

PAGE 75. RIGHTING A WRECKED LOCOMOTIVE. Soldier-photographer Andrew J. Russell recorded U.S. Military Railroad personnel attempting to right a locomotive derailed by marauding Confederates on Virginia's Manassas Gap Railroad. Most of Russell's photographs were intended as illustrations for instruction manuals issued to the Union's railroad corps.

PAGE 76. NAVAL EXPERIMENTAL BATTERY. Admiral John A. Dahlgren established an experimental battery on the grounds of the U.S. Insane Asylum near Washington to test-fire the latest in heavy-caliber naval ordnance. Photographed shortly after the end of the war, the battery included a British-manufactured Armstrong gun (center), a curiously shaped weapon that fired a 150-pound shell. This particular gun had been captured from Confederate forces at Fort Caswell, North Carolina.

PAGE 77. METHOD OF DESTROYING R.R. TIES AND RAILS. Andrew J. Russell documented a method both Union and Confederate troops used to destroy enemy rail communications. The rails were heated atop burning ties, and when red hot, bent from their own weight.

PAGE 78. UNION NAVAL OFFICERS (SHIP, PLACE, UNKNOWN). Federal naval officers gather on the deck of their vessel beside a large-caliber Parrott gun (right). The Union blockade of Southern ports and seizure of river arteries enforced an ever-tightening stranglehold on the embattled Confederacy.

PAGE 79. MORTAR SCHOONER AT ALEXANDRIA, VIRGINIA. The officers and crew of a U.S. naval schooner gather beside a huge mortar capable of lobbing 200-pound shells onto enemy positions. Because of their guns' elevated trajectory, mortar schooners were frequently employed in the bombardment of Confederate river defenses.

CANNON IN FORMER CONFEDERATE WORKS, ATLANTA. Positioned in the embrasure of a former Confederate earthwork, a Union cannon guards an encampment of General Sherman's victorious Yankees following the capture of Atlanta, Georgia. The fallen city is visible in the left background of George N. Barnard's photograph.

BATTLEFIELD OF MISSIONARY RIDGE. The denuded landscape of Missionary Ridge shows the effects of the fighting that raged there in November 1863. On November 25 the forces of U. S. Grant stormed and cleared the commanding elevation of Confederate soldiers. Carried away by their enthusiasm, the Union troops advanced beyond their planned objective and continued up the steep slope, breaking Braxton Bragg's siege of Chattanooga, and confirming Grant's reputation as the most successful Yankee commander of the war to date.

PAGE 85. CHATTANOOGA FROM LOOKOUT MOUNTAIN. In November 1863, the sheer rock face of Lookout Mountain, overlooking the Tennessee River and Chattanooga, was the setting for "the Battle above the Clouds"—the first in a string of victories by U. S. Grant over Braxton Bragg's Southern forces. The panoramic locale was a favorite for George N. Barnard and other photographers; one pair of enterprising cameramen set up a makeshift studio at the very edge of the precipice.

PAGE 86. BOULDER ON LOOKOUT MOUNTAIN. In November 1863, the rugged slopes of Lookout Mountain witnessed some of the bloodiest combat in Grant's successful attempt to break the Confederate siege of Chattanooga. But Barnard found the natural beauty of the mountain, with its clear ponds and graceful waterfall, more compelling than its military significance. He believed photography was a "necessary art . . . as much so as painting and sculpture." His views of Lu-La Lake and a lichen-covered boulder reflected his admiration for Britain's Pre-Raphaelite painters, whose belief in the divinity of nature was coupled with a fervent insistence on natural realism.

PAGE 87. LU-LA LAKE, LOOKOUT MOUNTAIN, TENNESSEE.

PAGE 88. LEE & GORDON'S MILLS, WEST CHICKAMAUGA CREEK, GEORGIA. Lee & Gordon's Mills, a dozen miles south of Chattanooga, was the site of the initial clash of arms in the two-day battle of Chickamauga (September 19–20, 1863). General William Rosecrans's Federal army was smashed by Bragg's Confederates in the bloodiest battle of the war's western theater.

PAGE 89. JOHN ROSS HOUSE, ROSSVILLE, GEORGIA. When Union troops retreated through Rossville Gap in the wake of their defeat at Chickamauga, John Ross's humble cabin became a blood-soaked field hospital, where military surgeons struggled to save the mangled wounded.

PAGE 91. KENNESAW MOUNTAIN, GEORGIA. In 1866, when photographer George N. Barnard revisited the battlefields of Sherman's Atlanta campaign, earthworks still scarred the scene of a costly Union repulse at Kennesaw Mountain. By the fourth year of the conflict, parade-ground tactics had begun to give way to the grim reality of trench warfare.

PAGE 92. BATTLEFIELD OF NEW HOPE CHURCH, GEORGIA. Nearly two years after the battle of New Hope Church, shell-torn trees and a crumbling Rebel breastwork remained on the Georgia hillside soldiers called "the Hell Hole." There General Joseph Johnston's Southern forces delayed Sherman's advance for an entire week in May 1864.

PAGE 93. BATTLEFIELD OF NEW HOPE CHURCH. Fighting from the cover of rifle pits and log traverses, Johnston's Confederates inflicted grievous losses on Sherman's men at New Hope Church. Sherman reported that "the whole country is one vast fort."

PAGE 94. ETOWAH RIVER DEFENSES, GEORGIA. Another Barnard image records abandoned Confederate defenses overlooking the Etowah River railroad bridge. Before evacuating the site on May 20, 1864, Johnston's men destroyed the span, but Yankee engineers quickly rebuilt the crossing of the river Sherman called "the Rubicon of Georgia."

PAGE 95. UNION SOLDIERS IN A CAPTURED CONFEDERATE FORT, ATLANTA, GEORGIA. In October 1864, victorious Federal soldiers rest beside the ramparts and bombproof dugout of a captured Confederate fort, part of the earthen defenses that ringed Atlanta, Georgia. After a series of bitter engagements, General John Bell Hood's Southern forces evacuated the city, paving the way for Sherman's March to the Sea.

PAGE 96. CONFEDERATE DEFENSES AT ATLANTA. Yankee troops man an abandoned Rebel artillery position in the Atlanta defenses. A line of rifle pits extends into the distance, screened by sharpened, interlocking logs called chevaux-de-frise.

PAGE 97. CAPTURED CONFEDERATE FORTIFICATIONS IN FRONT OF ATLANTA. A canteen hangs from the stacked muskets of Northern soldiers camped in a fallen strongpoint on the southwestern outskirts of Atlanta. The loss of Atlanta dealt a grievous blow to waning Confederate hopes.

RUINED ROUNDHOUSE, GEORGIA RAILROAD, ATLANTA, 1866. Locomotives parked surrealistically amid the shattered remnants of Atlanta's Georgia Railroad roundhouse testify to the devastation wrought by Sherman's relentless campaign. Before embarking on his March to the Sea, Sherman ordered the evacuation of Atlanta's civilian population and destroyed the city's transportation infrastructure.

RUINS OF THE HENRY HOUSE, BULL RUN. The war's first great land engagement, the battle of Bull Run, claimed the life of an elderly widow named Judith Henry, whose home stood at the epicenter of the fighting. Only a chimney and a few boards remained of the house when Union troops returned to the field eight months after the battle.

SOLDIERS' GRAVES AT BULL RUN. Crude headboards and a muddy slough mark the temporary resting place of soldiers slain in the first battle of Bull Run. Primitive field burials frequently made it impossible to identify the dead; tens of thousands were reinterred as unknowns.

EFFECTS OF A SHELL EXPLOSION, FREDERICKSBURG. General Herman Haupt (left), chief of the U.S. Military Railroad, surveys a shattered caisson and its slain horses following the second battle of Fredericksburg, in May 1863. The debris marked the position of the Washington Artillery of New Orleans, a unit that lost forty-five men and six guns in the fight.

UPPER LEFT. FALLEN CONFEDERATE AT DEVIL'S DEN, GETTYSBURG. Although Alexander Gardner identified this youthful casualty of the battle of Gettysburg as a slain sharpshooter, he was probably an infantryman from Hood's division who fell in the advance through Devil's Den. Gardner later dragged the corpse some forty yards, and exposed a more famous view of the fallen "sharpshooter."

LOWER LEFT. A HARVEST OF DEATH, GETTYSBURG. Stripped of weapons, accoutrements, and shoes, a group of Federal soldiers rest in what Alexander Gardner called "a Harvest of Death" at Gettysburg. Though the exact location of this view is open to conjecture, it is likely that these men fell as the Union Third Corps was driven from a position near the Emmitsburg Road on the second day of the battle.

UPPER RIGHT. DEAD CONFEDERATE SOLDIER NEAR PLUM RUN, GETTYSBURG. During his visit to the Gettysburg battlefield on July 6, 1863, Alexander Gardner photographed the bloated corpse of a Confederate soldier where he had fallen four days earlier in the assault on Little Round Top. So many men died in the rocky swale bordering Plum Run that the site was dubbed "the Slaughter Pen."

LOWER RIGHT. CONFEDERATE DEAD NEAR THE ROSE WOODS, GETTYSBURG. Gathered for mass burial by their victorious enemy, Confederate dead lie near the edge of the Rose Woods at Gettysburg. Regiments from Georgia and South Carolina suffered heavy losses at this point on July 2, 1863, as they advanced northeastward toward the infamous Wheatfield.

PAGE 107. DEAD CONFEDERATE SOLDIER IN THE TRENCHES OF FORT MAHONE, PETERSBURG, VIRGINIA. A young Confederate soldier lies sprawled in death in the trenches of Fort Mahone, following the climactic Union assault on Petersburg on April 3, 1865. Six days later, Robert E. Lee surrendered his army at Appomattox. This image is one of a series of photographs of slain defenders by Thomas C. Roche.

PAGE 108. BURIAL OF UNION DEAD AT FREDERICKSBURG, MAY 1864. In May 1864, a burial party inters Union dead in a military cemetery at Fredericksburg, Virginia. The town's war-ravaged homes served as hospitals for thousands of casualties from Grant's inexorable offensive against Lee's Army of Northern Virginia.

PAGE 109. BATTLEFIELD OF RINGGOLD, GEORGIA. On November 27, 1863, the village of Ringgold, Georgia (some fifteen miles southeast of Chattanooga) witnessed a determined stand by Confederate General Patrick Cleburne against a much larger Federal force. The Irish-born Cleburne, a veteran of the British army, was among the war's most inspirational field commanders.

SCENE OF GENERAL McPHERSON'S DEATH AT ATLANTA. On July 22, 1864, during the confused fighting that raged on the outskirts of Atlanta, Union Major General James B. McPherson was killed when he mistakenly rode into the Confederate lines. Commander of the Army of the Tennessee and Sherman's principal subordinate, McPherson was the highest-ranking Federal general to die in the war.

CONFEDERATE ENTRENCHMENTS AT ATLANTA. A dead horse lies below a hillside scarred by Confederate entrenchments overlooking the Western and Atlantic Railroad on the outskirts of Atlanta. Formidable as they were, the fortifications were unable to keep Sherman's army at bay.

ABANDONED CONFEDERATE FORTIFICATIONS AT CENTREVILLE, VIRGINIA, MARCH 1862. In March 1862, urged on by the impatient President Lincoln, General George McClellan's Army of the Potomac finally took the field against General Joseph Johnston's Confederate forces. When the Yankees reached the vicinity of Centreville, Virginia, they found that their foe had retreated southward, leaving behind formidable earthworks and abandoned winter huts.

CONFEDERATE PRISONERS ESCORTED BY UNION CAVALRY.
Guarded by Union cavalrymen, a vast column of Rebel prisoners marches
toward an uncertain future. Before 1864, captured soldiers stood a good chance
of being exchanged for comrades held by the opposing side. But the exchange
system broke down when the North determined to hold on to its prisoners,
draining the South of manpower in an increasingly grim war of attrition.

FORMER CONFEDERATE WORKS IN FRONT OF ATLANTA. A group of Union soldiers relax in their canvas tent while a comrade guards the rampart of a captured Rebel bastion in the defenses of Atlanta. Sherman's grizzled veterans were poised for the next step in the Union's effort to destroy the Confederacy: the March to the Sea.

CULPEPER, VIRGINIA. Like many Virginia communities, the town of Culpeper was swept by the ebb and flow of contending armies. In the summer of 1862 and again in 1863, Union occupiers were forced to abandon their position there, but by 1864 Culpeper was again in Yankee hands.

CENTREVILLE, VIRGINIA. Situated on a strategic plateau between Manassas and Washington, the battered and nearly deserted hamlet of Centreville, Virginia, witnessed the demoralized retreat of two Federal armies from the field of Bull Run in little more than a year's time. Most of the homes were commandeered as field hospitals for the wounded who had to be left behind.

COLONEL EMORY UPTON AND STAFF, WINTER 1863–64. During the winter of 1863–64, the elegant residence of the Major family, situated between the Hazel and Rappahannock rivers north of Culpeper, served as headquarters for Colonel Emory Upton's brigade of the Union Sixth Corps. Upton (who stands on the steps with members of his staff, visiting civilians, and two slave children) had graduated from West Point in May 1861. Despite his youth, his intrepid leadership won him promotion to general's rank in the summer of 1864.

PARADE TO DEDICATION OF SOLDIERS' NATIONAL CEMETERY, GETTYSBURG. On November 19, 1863, Union troops parade down Baltimore Street in Gettysburg, en route to the ceremonial dedication of the Soldiers' National Cemetery. In the four months following the battle, the remains of thirty-five hundred Federal dead had been reinterred there.

DEDICATION OF SOLDIERS' NATIONAL CEMETERY, GETTYSBURG. During the dedication of the Soldiers' National Cemetery, an honor guard of soldiers in full dress uniform stands "in place rest" while President Lincoln, Pennsylvania's governor, Andrew Curtin, and other dignitaries cluster on the speakers' platform (left background). Lincoln's brief address to the crowd was a stirring affirmation of national hope.

PAGE 126. BRIGADIER GENERAL WILLIAM W. BELKNAP AND ORDERLIES, 1865. Brigadier General William W. Belknap, a former Iowa attorney, sits between two of his staff orderlies. At the battle of Atlanta, the burly general single-handedly captured an enemy colonel, heaving the Confederate officer across the Union breastworks by his coat collar. Belknap later served as secretary of war in President Grant's administration, but his tenure was marred by charges of political corruption.

PAGE 127. BREVET BRIGADIER GENERAL CLINTON D. MACDOUGALL AND STAFF. Posing with his staff at war's end, Brevet Brigadier General Clinton D. MacDougall (seated second from left) was a twenty-five-year-old, Scottish-born brigade commander with a wealth of combat experience. The black armbands worn by several of the officers indicate that this image was taken shortly after President Lincoln's assassination. Their mud-spattered boots testify to the deplorable condition of Washington's city streets.

PAGE 129. RUINS OF RICHMOND, VIRGINIA, FROM THE CANAL BASIN, APRIL 1865. A Federal soldier stands beside abandoned Confederate ordnance following the Union occupation of Richmond, in April 1865. The columned portico of Virginia's state capitol, which also housed the Confederate Congress, overlooks the James River canal basin and blocks of fire-ravaged homes and businesses.

RUINS OF GALLEGO FLOUR MILLS, RICHMOND (PANORAMA). With a haunting, tragic beauty, the roofless and crumbling façades of Richmond's Gallego Flour Mills stand in mute testimony to the devastated hopes of the Confederacy. 1865.

RUINS OF THE PHILLIPS HOUSE NEAR FALMOUTH, VIRGINIA.
The gutted Phillips House near Falmouth, Virginia, was one of countless Southern homesteads destroyed in the course of the war. General Ambrose Burnside's headquarters during the battle of Fredericksburg, in December 1862, the mansion fell victim to a chimney fire in February of the following year.

RUINS OF CHARLESTON, SOUTH CAROLINA, 1865. No Confederate city held such symbolic value as Charleston, South Carolina. It was where the first shot of the war was fired, and the Union expended great effort and thousands of lives to capture it. But Charleston held out until the last months of the conflict, when Sherman's advancing forces compelled the evacuation of the Confederate garrison. By 1865, bombardment and fire had ravaged the once elegant city.

RUINS OF RICHMOND, 1865.

FORT SUMTER, CHARLESTON HARBOR, SOUTH CAROLINA. On the afternoon of April 14, 1865, the same Stars and Stripes that had been lowered four years earlier was raised again over the battered rubble of Fort Sumter. That evening, at a Washington theater, Abraham Lincoln became a final sacrifice to the war that claimed the lives of 620,000 Americans.

PLATES

PAGE 3. Attributed to Alexander Gardner. Chair in which President Lincoln was sitting when shot. 1865.

PAGE 5. Attributed to Alexander Gardner. The stage of Ford's Theatre, Washington, D.C. 1865.

PAGE 25. Attributed to S. R. Seibert. Distant view of Fort Sumter from the Confederate batteries at Fort Johnson, James Island, South Carolina. 1865. According to the official List of the Photographs and Photographic Negatives Relating to the War for the Union (Washington, D.C.: Government Printing Office, 1897), Seibert made between forty and sixty-three photographs "showing existing conditions of the more important points and defenses of Charleston, S.C." He is known to have made several images of the Confederate gun positions on Johnson's Island.

PAGE 27. Unidentified photographer. Engineer Camp, Eighth New York State Militia, Camp McDowell, Arlington Heights, Virginia. 1861. This image was copyrighted by Brady and published in his *Incidents of the War* series.

PAGE 29. Andrew J. Russell. Marye's Heights, Fredericksburg, Virginia. Confederate dead behind the stone wall. The Sixth Maine Infantry penetrated the Confederate lines at this point. 1863.

PAGES 30–31. Unidentified photographer. Unidentified officers and enlisted men of the Fourth Michigan Infantry. 1861.

PAGE 33. Unidentified photographer. Officers of the First Connecticut Heavy Artillery, Fort Richardson, Virginia. c. 1862.

PAGE 35. Unidentified photographer. Officers of the Fifty-fifth New York Infantry at Fort Gaines, near Tenley, New York. 1861.

PAGE 37. Unidentified photographer. Troops of the Second Pennsylvania Heavy Artillery, Fort Slemmer, Washington, D.C. 1861.

PAGE 39. Officers and Troopers of the Seventh New York Cavalry near Washington. 1861–62.

PAGE 41. Unidentified photographer. The Seventh Pennsylvania Reserves at drill near Langley, Virginia. c. 1861.

PAGE 43. Unidentified photographer. Union infantry camp. c. 1863.

PAGE 45. George N. Barnard. Pass in the Raccoon Range, Whiteside, Tennessee. No. 1. 1864. (Plate 6: *Photographic Views of Sherman's Campaign.*)

PAGE 47. Attributed to A. J. Russell. Officers of the 164th and 170th New York Infantry regiments at a woodcutters' camp on the Orange and Alexandria Railroad in northern Virginia. c. 1864.

PAGE 48. Unidentified photographer. Union officer in his camp quarters. c. 1864.

PAGE 49. Unidentified photographer. Commissary tent with hanging beef. c. 1864.

PAGE 50. Unidentified photographer. "Between Decks On a Transport." c. 1864.

PAGE 51. Unidentified photographer. Military hospital, near Washington, D.C. 1864.

PAGE 52. Unidentified photographer. A freedmen's village. c. 1863.

PAGE 53. Attributed to Andrew J. Russell. Camp of the U.S. Military Railroad's construction corps near City Point, Virginia. 1864.

PAGE 55. Unidentified photographer. View of Chattanooga, Tennessee. c. 1864.

PAGE 57. Andrew J. Russell. Stockade built by order of General Herman Haupt for the protection of government property, enclosing the machine shops and yard of the Orange and Alexandria Railroad. c. 1863.

PAGE 58. Attributed to Andrew J. Russell. Contraband laborers, Alexandria Wharf, Virginia. c. 1864.

PAGE 59. Andrew J. Russell. Upper Wharf, Belle Plain, Virginia, laid by the Engineer Corps. 1864.

PAGE 60. Attributed to Andrew J. Russell. Docked Union supply ship at White House Landing on the Pamunkey River. c. 1864.

PAGE 61. Unidentified photographer. The Union monitor *Saugus* on the James River. c. 1864.

PAGE 63. Attributed to Thomas C. Roche. Fortifications and bombproofs in front of Petersburg, Virginia. 1865. (Published as No. 3336, E. & H. T. Anthony & Co. series *War Views*, from negative by Brady & Co., Washington, D.C.)

PAGE 65. Unidentified photographer. Government corral, near Fort Carroll, at Giesboro Point, Washington, D.C. c. 1863.

PAGE 67. Attributed to Andrew J. Russell. U.S. Military Railroad tracks at approach to Union Mills, Virginia. c. 1863.

PAGE 68. Unidentified photographer. Union transport steamer *Missionary* on the Tennessee River. c. 1864.

PAGE 69. Andrew J. Russell. Scene of the explosion, City Point, Virginia, August 1864.

PAGE 70. Attributed to Andrew J. Russell. The military bridge at Union Mills, Virginia. c. 1863.

PAGE 71. George N. Barnard. Trestle Bridge at Whiteside. 1864. (Plate 4: *Photographic Views of Sherman's Campaign.*)

PAGE 73. George N. Barnard. Ruins of Hood's Ordnance Train. 1864. (Plate 44: *Photographic Views of Sherman's Campaign.*)

PAGE 75. Andrew J. Russell. Wreck on the Manassas Gap Railroad. The track had been torn up by Confederates. c. 1863.

PAGE 76. Unidentified photographer. Naval guns in the experimental battery on the grounds of the U.S. Insane Asylum. c. 1865.

PAGE 77. Andrew J. Russell. "How Sherman's Boys Fixed the Rail Road." c. 1863.

PAGE 78. Unidentified photographer. Union naval officers (ship, place, unknown). c. 1864.

PAGE 79. Unidentified photographer. U.S. Naval Gunboat at Alexandria. c. 1864.

PAGE 81. George N. Barnard. Cannon in former Confederate works, Atlanta. 1864.

PAGE 83. Unidentified photographer. View of the battlefield of Missionary Ridge. c. 1864.

PAGE 85. George N. Barnard. Chattanooga Valley from Lookout Mountain, No. 2. 1864 or 1866. (Plate 14: *Photographic Views of Sherman's Campaign.*)

PAGE 86. Attributed to George N. Barnard. Bluff 1,299 feet high, Lookout Mountain, Tennessee. 1864 or 1866.

PAGE 87. George N. Barnard. Lu-La Lake, Lookout Mountain. (Plate 15: *Photographic Views of Sherman's Campaign.*)

PAGE 88. Attributed to George N. Barnard. Lee & Gordon's Mills, West Chickamauga Creek, Georgia, near the Chickamauga battlefield. c. 1866.

PAGE 89. George N. Barnard. John Ross House. 1866. (Plate 16: *Photographic Views of Sherman's Campaign.*)

PAGE 91. George N. Barnard. The Front of Kennesaw Mountain, Georgia. 1866. (Plate 31: *Photographic Views of Sherman's Campaign.*)

PAGE 92. George N. Barnard. Battlefield of New Hope Church, Georgia, No. 1. 1866. (Plate 25: *Photographic Views of Sherman's Campaign.*)

PAGE 93. George N. Barnard. Battlefield of New Hope Church, Georgia, No. 2. 1866. (Plate 26: *Photographic Views of Sherman's Campaign.*)

PAGE 94. George N. Barnard. Allatoona from the Etowah. 1866. (Plate 24: *Photographic Views of Sherman's Campaign.*)

PAGE 95. George N. Barnard. Atlanta, Georgia. View from casemated Confederate fort looking north toward W.A.R.R. (Western and Atlantic Railroad). 1864.

PAGE 96. George N. Barnard. Rebel works in front of Atlanta. 1864.

PAGE 97. George N. Barnard. Rebel Works in Front of Atlanta, Georgia, No. 5. 1864. (Plate 43: *Photographic Views of Sherman's Campaign.*)

PAGE 99. George N. Barnard. City of Atlanta, No. 1. 1866. (Plate 4: *Photographic Views of Sherman's Campaign.*)

PAGE 100. George N. Barnard. Ruins of Mrs. Henry's House, Battlefield of Bull Run. 1862.

PAGE 101. George N. Barnard. Soldiers' Graves, Bull Run. 1862.

PAGE 103. Andrew J. Russell. Havoc. Effects of a 32-pound shell from gun of Second Massachusetts Heavy Artillery, Fredericksburg, Virginia. 1863.

PAGE 105 (UPPER LEFT). Alexander Gardner. A Sharpshooter's Last Sleep, Gettysburg, July 6, 1863. (Plate 49: *Gardner's Photographic Sketch Book of the War.*)

PAGE 105 (UPPER RIGHT). Alexander Gardner. Fallen Confederate sharpshooter at foot of Round Top, Gettysburg. July 6, 1863.

PAGE 105 (LOWER LEFT). Timothy O'Sullivan. A Harvest of Death, Gettysburg, July 1863. (Plate 37: *Gardner's Photographic Sketch Book of the War.*)

PAGE 105 (LOWER RIGHT). James F. Gibson. Confederate dead laid out for burial, Gettysburg. July 1863.

PAGE 107. Thomas C. Roche. A dead Rebel soldier as he lay in the trenches of Fort Mahone, called by the soldiers "Fort Damnation." This view was taken the morning after the storming of Petersburg, Virginia. 1865.

PAGE 108. Unidentified photographer. Burial of Union soldiers at Fredericksburg, Virginia. 1864.

PAGE 109. George N. Barnard. Battlefield of Ringgold, Georgia. 1865.

PAGE 111. George N. Barnard. Scene of General McPherson's Death. 1864 or 1866. (Plate 35: *Photographic Views of Sherman's Campaign.*)

PAGE 113. George N. Barnard. Confederate lines, battlefield of Atlanta, Georgia. 1864.

PAGE 115. George N. Barnard and James F. Gibson. Fortifications on the heights of Centreville, Virginia. March 1862.

ACKNOWLEDGMENTS

Publication of this book would not have been realized without the
expert advice and generosity of Edward A. Miller.
Victoria Wilson's understanding and tireless support, as well as her
suggestions, were essential to preparation and production of the book.
Katherine Hourigan's careful attention to editorial detail
and Karen Mugler's production editing were also beneficial.
Tina Davis's elegant design and Robert Hennessey's superb tritone
separations greatly enhance our appreciation of the photographs.

Developed, prepared, and produced by

Constance Sullivan Editions

Design and typography by Tina Davis, New York

Printed by Meridian Printing Company, East Greenwich, Rhode Island

Bound by Horowitz / Rae, Fairfield, New Jersey

Tritone separations were made by Robert H. Hennessey

from the original albumen prints